Bernie

A Story for
Someone Who
Thinks They Might
Like to Have a Dog

Cork Eringaard

Bernie
A STORY FOR SOMEONE WHO THINKS THEY MIGHT LIKE TO HAVE A DOG

iUniverse books may be ordered through booksellers or by contacting:

iUniverse
1663 Liberty Drive
Bloomington, IN 47403
www.iuniverse.com
844-349-9409

ISBN: 978-1-6632-0862-0 (sc)
ISBN: 978-1-6632-0863-7 (e)

Library of Congress Control Number: 2020925087

Print information available on the last page.

iUniverse rev. date: 01/15/2021

Bernie

The Story of the Many Adventures of Bernie

Cork Eringaard

When Bernie Was a Puppy

I first came to know we had something special when Bernie came with us for the first time to open the cottage for the summer. It was spring, and the neighbors were back.

We could anticipate visits by the free-ranging dogs who would appear at the sliding-glass doors of our lakeside cottage. The dogs came to say hello and for the expected treat, a habit they developed last summer.

Until now, Bernie was a normal puppy, managing to do what puppies do—chew my wife's slippers, my daughter's shoes, the house molding, the car's center console, and the leather on my reading chair. Of course that is to be expected if you leave a pup unattended for any time at all. We anticipated that sort of thing, but one is never quite prepared for it when it happens.

He learned his name quickly. Perhaps because it was election time, he heard the name Bernie around the house a lot at naming time.

He was potty trained quickly too. We lived for a while aboard a sailboat with two small dogs and found it difficult to go ashore at convenient times. Sometimes we found ourselves at anchor and unable to get ashore till the next day. So for these reasons, we trained the dogs to use hospital diaper pads. Now you can buy them in pet supply stores. City living also encouraged us to use diaper pads with Bernie.

We know another dog called Ella. He looked to be saying, "I am back. Do you have a treat for me?" Bernie saw the dog first. This was the first big dog he had ever seen. He was standing with his front paw planted. The other paw he pointed at the dog in the doorway and barked as if to say, "See what I see? Look at what is out there."

During Bernie's first summer, there were more dogs to meet. They gathered in cottage yards along the lakeshore. Bernie readily joined the group to have a dog. Maybe a dog just like Bernie?

Growing up, Bernie, like all our previous dogs, had many pet shop doggy toys. The idea was hopefully to avoid the destruction of items like shoes, slippers, hankies, and socks.

The toys were picked up every evening and stored in his kennel. And each morning Bernie carefully removed every one of them, scattering them everywhere around the kitchen. At night, all were collected and again stored in the kennel. Of course this was followed by a morning wake-up followed by a redistribution.

Bernie's favorite toy was a tennis ball. One could throw the ball either indoors or outdoors, and Bernie never tired of retrieving it.

Two games are involved here. In the first one, Bernie gave give me the ball, but I would have to throw it quickly so that he could go get it again. The second game was to retrieve the ball but be reluctant to release the ball. This last often resulted in a tussle for the ball. One learns Bernie has a powerful bite.

Bernie Plays Golf

About the same time, my neighbor Tom and I were planning on playing in a golf tournament. So he decided some practice would be a good idea. Not to be discouraged by the grass cutting, he used his short irons to hit golf balls in an area unencumbered by a lawn-mowing tractor. Bernie, on his own while sniffing around, saw Tom hit his first shot. Bernie was off running and retrieved Tom's golf ball. Tom hit that ball again, and Bernie brought it back again. This happened time after time.

Tom bought a whole bucket of balls but only used one. Bernie brought that one ball back fifty-three times! Tom said, "If I knew that Bernie was going to be here, I would not have bought a whole bucket of golf balls."

When it came to hitting the long ball, Bernie did not do as well. By now he was a bit tired. Besides, it took too long to find and retrieve what was hit so far out. I was convinced that my golf ball–hitting skills had atrophied over the years and that I should not play in the tournament. Bernie, a very tired dog, and I headed for home.

Lost Dog

Ball retrieving was really the start of something. When Bernie was not yet a year old, I observed another of his chasing skills.

It was on a wet snowy day. The snow was six inches or so deep. Nearing the end of our daily walk, Bernie startled a small deer. Bernie gave chase immediately.

Not heeding any of my commands to come, stay, or anything else I called in my effort to end the chase, he disappeared into the surrounding woods. That day I learned the command, "Come, Bernie," did not work well when he was distracted. I tried to follow him, but a heavy wet snow was falling and quickly obliterated his tracks. I lost him.

I spent about an hour looking for him, following the roads that surrounded the woods in which he disappeared.

I was worried as it would be dark soon. So I engaged the assistance of some maintenance workers heading home for the evening. They drove around, combing the area.

With the use of the workers' vehicles, we were able to widened the search area. While they drove, I went looking down a street of houses located on the lake, calling as I went. I stopped one house short of the end of the street and returned to where I first lost Bernie.

It was getting dark, and I was distraught. I wanted to leave my jacket on the ground on the spot I lost him. I learned that trick when as a boy. I lost my basset hound, who took off to chase a deer we encountered on an afternoon walk in the Manistee National Forest. I left my jacket on the ground where I last saw him and found him sleeping on it the next morning.

Coming toward me was a truck, its lights blinking, its horn honking. When the truck reached me, one of the guys told me excitedly, "We found Bernie!"

After expressing the appropriate gratitude and giving Bernie all kinds of welcoming hugs, I asked, "Where did you find him?"

The driver answered, "He was lying down next to a big rock, totally exhausted. Heavy wet snow was clinging to all his rather thick long hair."

The house where they found was the last house on the street I searched. I had just missed seeing him.

I was much relieved to have Bernie back. And if you continue reading, you will find Bernie and I have had a number of adventures since, but not nearly as frightening to me as this one was. We live in kind of a deer park, and there have been many deer chases. But now Bernie listens and comes when he is called, though not always instantaneously. But one thing he has learned is, "Come, Bernie."

Most recently he has been learning to respond to a whistle, ending my need to call, "Come, Bernie" whenever he wanders out of sight too long. Much to the relief of the neighbors, who heard me often shout, "Come, Bernie." A whistle or whistling is much less obtrusive. I use both methods, an actual whistle when I think to bring it along. But he seems to like me to call him with the bobwhite chirp.

Boats

There was a time when Bernie liked boat rides. He liked the pleasure rides with our twin daughters. Or when I went fishing, it was usually just Bernie and me. He would ride near the bow, two feet on the gunnel, watching the shoreline and letting me know whether there were creatures—human or otherwise—to be seen as we slowly made our way.

This willingness to accompany me ended abruptly when I asked Bernie to board a new boat we recently obtained. Bernie accidentally fell off the dock when he tried to board.

Let me try to explain. Our owner's association has a leash law: all dogs must be on a leash when on the premises. Bernie lives here all year, not just summers, when more people are here. For most of the year he runs without a leash. It's in the summer months—June, July, August, and parts of May and September—he is on the leash except when we go into the woods or adjacent neighborhoods.

There is a leash rule on the books, but nothing in the rule book says someone has to be holding the leash. So you often find Bernie running around with a leash but no holder of said leash. Bernie is an inordinately friendly dog who says hello to everyone. Some people not in the know think Bernie escaped and bring him back to me.

It is the dragging of his leash that started his boating reluctance. We were down at the boat. I was putting fishing gear aboard when Bernie was getting ready to board. Then the leash that he was dragging got caught on a dock cleat. When Bernie tried to jump aboard, the caught leash caused him to fall between the dock and the boat. Hanging there half in and out of the water is an experience Bernie well remembers.

He shows the same angst when it is time to get off the boat. He wants off, but he urges me to lift him off the boat long before I am ready to leave. I still need to clean up and stow things, but Bernie wants off. So I carefully lift him out and put him on the finger peer attached to the dock.

Bernie does not trust the getting-off-the-boat process any more than the getting-on-the-boat process. I tell him to go to the golf cart. This is the vehicle we drive from the cottage to the boat with all our gear. He will then traipse by fifteen boat slips, find a shady place on the golf cart, and patiently wait for me.

This he will do except for when there are a large number of seagulls or Canadian geese roosting on the flagpole grounds adjacent to dock parking. He charges into the birds, forcing them to take flight—which is always fun to see—before returning to the golf cart to wait for me.

More Chasing Skills

It is on our walks and around the bird feeders that Bernie enhanced his chasing skills. The bird feeders introduced him to chipmunks, red squirrels, ground squirrels, shrews, and fox squirrels. We saw them in the wooded area all around our place, under walnut trees, oak trees, and berry trees. We walked these areas often, and Bernie came to know all the good spots in which to look.

On one of those occasions, I stopped to talk to a neighbor. Bernie caught a chipmunk, brought it to me, and placed it at feet my feet. It was still alive, so it ran away. Bernie chased it and caught it again. This time I set it free and held onto Bernie so the chipmunk could get away safely.

The other day Bernie bought me a rather large creature I had not seen very often. It turned out to be an opossum, a rather large one, with interesting teeth. I told Bernie, "I really did not need a dead opossum." I managed to pick it up by its tail and flung it as far as I could back into the woods.

Not long after, Bernie reappeared with the same opossum. I again took it by the tail. This time I realized I was holding a live opossum. Remembering the teeth this fellow had, I put Bernie in the cottage and sent our guest in a different direction.

Been Here Before

It is probably true that in our nearly daily one- to three-mile walks Bernie has become accustomed to the neighborhood no matter what path we take. He knows the good spots to investigate. And he knows when I might stop to talk to a neighbor who might be ready to give him a treat if he were to stop by to say hello.

More important to him, he knows when going off the path means he might encounter a rodent, rabbit, or deer, so he is always looking, visiting the same spots over and over along the way. He knows where the friendly dogs are and where he might encounter those rather curious creatures—at least to Bernie—cats.

One path we take is along the lakeshore in an older cottage area. We usually go that way midday. In middle of summer, there are usually lots of people to see along the way.

Bernie gets thirsty and wants to drink out of the lake. But he is reluctant to get near the shore, where there might be waves. It doesn't matter how minor the lapping waves are, Bernie doesn't like them.

We know Bernie can swim because the family snuck him into the association swimming pool one night. He managed quit well when he had to, but he still was very reluctant. He actually has big paws, and if you did not know better, you would think he had webbed feet.

Before he will drink from the lake, he is patient enough to find a rock or some other obstruction that will block the slightest ripple.

My struggle is to keep him out of the muddy water on the other side of the road. Bernie prefers it because he does not have contend with ripples in the water.

See Any Deer?

Becoming aware of where we are also occurs when we are driving in the car. Bernie is usually asleep somewhere in the car away from the heater. But when we get near the neighborhoods where we have walked frequently, he seems to intuit proximity, wakes from his slumber, and begins watching out the window.

If you ask, "See any deer?" he becomes very attentive. He puts both front feet on the car's windowsill and presses his nose to the window. It happens every time.

On one occasion we saw a deer. It was standing near one of our familiar walking paths. No sooner did I stop and say, "See the deer," than Bernie was out the window and giving chase.

I have since learned to keep the window up partially, no matter how nice the day.

Over the last several years in my neighborhood, I have run into or have had deer run into my car five times. But since Bernie has become my deer spotter, I have not run into any deer.

The Big Dogs

Sometimes on our walks, checking out his various spots takes considerable time. Bernie tends to fall behind. I am inclined to continue walking, and that requires him to catch up to me. As I mentioned earlier, I used to call, "Come, Bernie," sometimes over and over again to the annoyance of any adult in listening range. I have learned to whistle a bobwhite call or just blow a whistle when it is time to move on.

I mention this because one of our neighbors who has a house a mile down our trail bought two German Shepherd puppies. Our walks in that direction required a stop, some rough play, and a treat before continuing our walk. Bernie always anticipated this, and as we drew closer to the house with the big dogs, his pace quickened.

Someone once told me, "Bernie is a big dog in a small body." By nine months he was full size. The German shepherds really grew and grew. They became really big dogs, bigger by far than the average Seeing Eye dog, probably half again that size.

Roughhousing was no longer fun for Bernie. The closer we got in our walks to their house, the less inclined he was to get ahead of me. He'd rather stay close by my side. There was no inclination to venture out where he might encounter trouble from those bullying dogs.

Now, as we get closer to the big dogs' house and they do not appear in their yard and there is no barking from the house, Bernie gets braver and ventures out to explore the yard. He leaves little markers around that say, "Bernie was here."

One day when passing the big dogs' house we found the dogs in their front yard. The owners, Franz and his wife, Sue, were there too. Between the three of us we were able to calm the dogs. For reasons I do not now remember, I was invited into the house. Moments later, Franz came into the house with the two big dogs but no Bernie.

Bernie was invited in, too, but despite the possibility of a treat, he had no interest. I told everybody, "Don't worry. He'll wait outside till I leave. Don't worry about him."

After a short time, probably close to a half hour, I was ready to leave. I went to the door and called for Bernie. No Bernie appeared. I set out to head home, calling, "Bernie," whistling the bobwhite song, and using my dog whistle. Still no Bernie.

By now I was getting worried. Where was Bernie? As I made my way home, I checked all the rodent spots he checked out on our walks, but still no Bernie. Maybe he had continued the walk without me and had kept going in the other direction. He sure knew that direction as well.

I was going to get the car so that I could cover a lot more territory looking for my lost dog than I could by walking. By now I was very concerned about Bernie's whereabouts.

Rounding the bend in the road before my house, what did I see? A dog sitting on its haunches behind my car, which was parked in the garage. It was Bernie! He was very relaxed and had a look on his face that seemed to be asking me, "What took you so long?"

While on Our Walks

On our walks, I always worry when Bernie is out of sight for a while. I worry about what he might be getting into or what is he eating. Not carrion, I hope. That could result in vomiting later in the day or into the evening. Carrion are the remains of a decaying bird, fish, or mammal. Some dogs like to roll in carrion as well. Bernie is one of those dogs unless he is watched closely.

When it happens, it requires a bath before he is allowed back in the house. And especially at bedtime because he has a tendency to climb into bed with you during the night. To no one's surprise, it does happen from time to time, and I end up giving dog baths at the most undesirable moments.

We do have eagles. One day after fishing, I asked Bernie to go to the golf cart. He had started on his way when I noticed an eagle overhead, his eye on the small creature below. That small creature was Bernie. I stopped what I was doing on the boat, grabbed a boat hook, and followed Bernie to the golf cart with my eye to the sky. I stayed with Bernie till I was sure the eagle had taken flight to other hunting grounds.

Foxes pass through our yard from time to time. Most foxes are thin, lightweight creatures that do not scare me should Bernie encounter one. I have wrestled with Bernie often in an effort to get tennis balls out of his mouth and been accidentally bitten. Since he has very strong jaws, the foxes did not worry me much till I happened to see two mating in our backyard. I realized one fox was actually the size of a very mature coyote. It was the biggest fox I had ever seen. Now I worry a bit. That is one fox I do not want Bernie to meet.

Skunks and Porcupines

Then there are also porcupines and skunks to worry about. One night a neighboring cottager stopped by to borrow something; I do not remember what. When I opened the sliding-glass door, Bernie scooted out into the night. After the neighbor left, Bernie came back rather quickly for him, I thought. And then I noticed he was sick. As it turned out, he was very sick.

He was regurgitating frequently. Whatever he had gotten into ended up all over the cottage floor, not waiting to get to his paper. I sat in my chair by the fireplace, holding Bernie in my lap until two in the morning. Then we crawled into bed together, me still holding him close, promising myself to take him to the veterinarian first thing in the morning. By morning things had improved some, but I decided to head to the vet anyway.

When I arrived, I left Bernie in the car and went into the office to see if they had time to see him. If not, then when would they have time to see him? The reception room was crowded with customers and staff.

When I got into the office, I heard one of the staff at the front say, "Oh, oh! Someone has encountered a skunk." Everyone was looking at me. I smelled like the skunk. They were talking about me. I did not have any inclination that I had a problem of that sort.

The vet and his staff came out to the car to inspect Bernie. At first they did not detect the smell on Bernie. But then they looked at his face. He apparently was sprayed in the head, and that accounted for his sickness last evening. I really smelled, and so did my clothes, my car, my bed, my blankets, the chair, and the couch. In other words, anywhere Bernie and I had gone had been left with a distinguished odor. After buying the appropriate soaps to wash my dog, clothes, and surfaces, I googled homemade recipes. It took three days to wash and then rewash everything, again and again, to return some normalcy to our place.

A Needle-Nosed Plier

One day not long after the skunk encounter, we were walking, and Bernie was, as usual, ranging out and exploring somewhere off our path. And he disappeared, again. Being out of sight for a little longer than usual, and with no clue as to where he might be, I called, "Come, Bernie," and blew my whistle. When he didn't show up, I thought, *Oh, no! Now what?*

Finally, as I drew closer to home, Bernie appeared, looking kind of bedraggled and funny like. As he got closer, I reached down to pet him. I realized what I saw was not the result of a carrion encounter but that of a porcupine. His face was full of porcupine quills.

About two years before Bernie, I was coming home from a trout fishing trip on the Bear River. Traveling on a backcountry road, I saw several vehicles parked on the road ahead of me. I stopped, got out of the car, and asked, "What's happening?"

Someone said that a bear was going to cross the road not far behind where I was parked. "If you want to see a bear, you should stick around." And then he asked, "Do you hear the dogs? They are trailing a bear."

The dogs belonged to these fellas. They were running their dogs with no interest in shooting the bear. The chase was on, and I listened.

All of sudden there was a change in tone of the dogs' barking. One of the fellas said, "Oh, no! It sounds like they have treed the bear."

Moments later, the pitch changed entirely. "I do not like the sound of that," the guy said. "Sounds like they got into a porcupine." Apparently as the bear went up the tree, the porcupine decided it was time to get out of the tree and fell right at the feet of the dogs.

They called their dogs in, and I spent the next two hours holding dogs while they extracted porcupine quills from their mouths, lips, tongues, gums, and faces.

I made some friends that day.

I tell this story because when I saw Bernie, I said to myself, "I can do this." I took Bernie back to the cottage and placed him on his favorite dog mattress, which I put on my favorite easy chair. I proceeded to pull out twenty-three quills. Pulling them out at first does hurt, but as we progressed, Bernie relaxed more and more. I accomplished the removal of all the quills in good time, except for three rather small obscure ones I discovered the next day.

The reason the quills came out so easily was because of a needle-nosed plier I used. When a quill was squished, it tended to release air pressure, making the extraction easier. In effect, puncturing the quill before pulling is the secret.

I think—or I hope anyway—he knows not tangle to with a porcupine in the future. They are still around, but I know of no other encounters.

Squirrels

Bernie likes to look for squirrels of all kinds—fox, red, and ground squirrels. He loves to give chase and tries to catch them. He has at times come very close to succeeding. When he encounters a squirrel on walks, he will chase it up a tree, and then standing at the tree's bottom, he barks at the treed squirrel. Using his forepaws, it looks like he is going to climb the tree. Bernie circles the tree while the squirrel watches and scolds him with angry chatter, probably complaining because of his efforts to collect stores for winter were being interrupted.

If I were a squirrel hunter, Bernie would be the perfect dog. The squirrel moves around the tree as Bernie moves around the tree; the squirrel is oblivious to me, the pretend hunter. I am not a hunter. Not anymore anyway.

How Bernie runs might explain his chasing capabilities. When trotting, he walks much like a fox does. The two feet on the left are synchronized alternately with the two feet on the right. It appears to me that two feet are momentarily on the ground while the two alternate feet are in motion.

However, when Bernie is really chasing something, he shifts into an entirely different way of running, more like a rabbit or maybe a kangaroo. His hind feet now move forward at the same time, as if they are trying to catch his front two feet, which are synchronized to move forward as it appears his rear feet are going to catch them.

I should add a caveat here. You might see Bernie looking at you from a sitting position. He has a habit of holding one paw out, like he wants to shake your hand. That characteristic comes into play when Bernie is in full chase. With one paw on the ground and the other held up, he can pivot into a ninety-degree turn without slowing down. This and the bunny hop serve Bernie well in any chase.

Bernie usually lets us know if we have a squirrel around the bird feeders, usually midmorning. Not so many of them in the summer and early fall, just enough to pique his interest. But as winter closes in, six or seven might appear regularly at about that time.

Once I saw a squirrel walk by our sliding-glass door off the living room. To me it seemed to look in and scratch the window to get Bernie barking. It was then I realized those squirrels like to tease Bernie and set him off barking.

Squirrel Game

The game of squirrel becomes more intense as winter descends. The ground is blanketed with snow and there are more visiting birds of all kinds, sitting in trees because there is no room for them at the feeders. Bernie is beside himself to get out there and give chase.

We open the sliding-glass doors, and he is off and chasing squirrels that run in all directions to get away. Bernie often trees them down by the lakeshore.

One day not long ago there were two squirrels by the bird feeders. Bernie barked, and I let him out. One of the squirrels went up the tree with the bird feeder, and the other ran for the tree down by the lake with Bernie close behind. The squirrel that went up the tree came down and chased after Bernie. Bernie somehow saw the second squirrel following him, did the Coton pivot, and began chasing the second squirrel.

Either that was an effort to serve as a decoy to save the first squirrel, or this was two squirrels in cahoots to tease Bernie. I think it was a tease. I say that because of what happened several days later.

One morning Bernie was sitting in his chair, which gives him a good view of the yard where the bird feeders are hung. I noticed one squirrel walk by the sliding-glass door. Bernie saw it but did not make a sound. I know he saw it because of his moving tail.

A few moments later, six more fox squirrels were on and under the feeders. Bernie became animated, scratching the sliding-glass door and barking to be let out of the house. When the door was opened, Bernie gave chase to the squirrels.

A squirrel clinging to the glass feeder lost his grip and fell at Bernie's feet. Bernie missed catching it by the tail by less than an inch. That squirrel headed for the tree down by the lake with Bernie in very close pursuit. Then all six squirrels climbed down out of the tree and proceeded to chase Bernie. The chased squirrel made it to the lake tree.

Bernie sensed what was happening behind him. In squirrel heaven, he did the Coton pivot and chased the other six to different trees located on the area grounds. I am convinced the squirrels' effort to tease Bernie became a near disaster, which they salvaged with the subsequent six-squirrel chase.

Bernie Cues Bingo

Bernie has a brother, not from the same litter at birth but from the same parents. Though Bingo is a year younger, he has many of Bernie's characteristics and mannerisms. When Bingo visits here on the lake, the two of them play a lot, tussle, and get a lot of attention from the adults around.

The walks I take with Bernie now mean two dogs to walk. Bernie knows the neighborhood, and I believe he takes pleasure showing Bingo all his favorite places to find things or where he has found things alive or decomposing in the past. I believe Bernie is teaching Bingo how to hunt. Cotons were, to my knowledge, never bred to be hunting dogs but rather to be playful lap dogs.

The two of them have been good partners in the woods. They stick together, which makes my walks with them easier.

Bingo has learned squirrels climb trees, red squirrels and chipmunks live in the rock fences that are found all around our place, and it's okay to bark at them.

Bernie Rescues Bingo

It was on one of these walks, this time with my wife, Sue and one twin daughter Emily home from college. The dogs were doing their thing, nosing around, looking for whatever. We had walked for about a mile and were getting close to the big dogs' house. Bernie, as usual, hung back with me, whereas Mom and daughter walked on ahead following Bingo

Bingo bounded ahead. When we got close to the big dogs' yard, Bingo spotted them at the same time they spotted him. Off Bingo went, tail a wagging. I have got to say in the main those German shepherds are really good dogs, friendly and very obedient for young dogs. They are just bigger and have lots of exuberance.

The big dogs, with their tails wagging, set out to greet and play with Bingo. It was not long before the play became rather rough, and Bingo let out yelps of panic.

Bernie watched, heard the crying, and saw Bingo's difficulty. Perhaps it was the lesson Bernie learned when he caught a squirrel he was chasing, and the other squirrels came out of the tree and chased him to save the threatened squirrel. Or maybe it all looked like too much fun, and he did not want miss the action. Whatever the reason, Bernie charged into the maelstrom as if to save Bingo. Now four dogs were roughhousing with all the sound and fury before the adults got them separated and quieted down again.

Once calmed, the dogs made friends while being restrained by Sue. Bernie and Bingo were soon back on their walk as if nothing happened.

At Home

Bernie loves to have his ears, jaw, and neck rubbed when he lies on his back. He sometimes sleeps on his back too. Bernie also sleeps on his stomach with all four feet stuck out in different directions. His favorite sleeping position is curling up like a ball whether next to me or a pillow.

He will tell you he wants his ears, jaw, and neck rubbed by holding up his front paw while sitting in front of you. If he has already crawled into my lap, he will tell me by poking my hand with his nose or paw.

I might want to take a short nap on the couch, and he wants my attention. He has a way of jumping and landing on me, which is startling when not expected. The same can be said of an unanticipated arrival in my lap when trying to read, or even if I've fallen asleep while reading. All these characteristics are lovable.

There are many other characteristics and mannerisms not mentioned. All of them combine to make having a Bernie at this stage of my life a wonderful adventure. I recommend it whether you are young or lot older. If you have the time, place, and resources to have a dog, have one.

Bernie's younger brother, Bingo

The neighborhood fox Bernie has avoided meeting

Deer visiting feeders attached to the squirrel tree

Postscript

Bernie is a Coton de Tulear, a small breed of dog named after the coastal city of Toliara, on the island of Madagascar, the third-largest island in the world, located off the southeast coast of Africa. The origin of the breed has only been recognized since the early 1970s by both the European and American kennel associations and only very recently recognized by the American Kennel Club. The story of its origins involves sixteenth- or seventeenth-century pirates, a sinking ship, an ocean survival, and breeding with indigenous island dogs, resulting in a very small and playful dog. It is considered the royal dog of Madagascar and has been commemorated with a Republic of Madagascar stamp.

All-white was once the preferred color of a Coton de Tulear, but black-and-white and tricolored Cotons have become popular recently. Its fur has a cottonlike texture, hence the name "Coton," pronounced like the French say "cotton." It is a dog that does not shed hair, save for puppy hair, and is hypoallergenic. It is a relatively healthy breed. Cotons love exercise, long walks, and lots of running. They like to impress and will sit up and walk on two legs. They really want to please, are extremely friendly, and work well with youngsters.

A beginning source for more information is wikipedia.org. A small but good bibliography can be found there through which much more can be learned.

Printed in the United States
By Bookmasters